Book about farts... ✓
Book about trumps... ✓
Book about snotty soup... ✓

Hmmmm. What should my next book be about...?

Suggestions welcome - message me on socials or email

First published in the UK in 2024
by Fiona Woodhead from FiandBooks.com
67 The Hollins, Triangle, Halifax, West Yorkshire. HX6 3LU.
www.fiandbooks.com
ISBN 978-1-909515-64-2

Copyright © 2024 by Lynsey Calvert
lcalvert1977@gmail.com
First edition printed November 2024
All rights reserved. Printed in the UK

Harry woke up with a nose full of snot.

AAAACCCHHHHOOOOO!

Hotdog jumped up in fright and ran off.

"Harry, are you okay?" his mum asked as she poked her head round the door.

"I don't feel well," Harry squeaked.

"I'll go and make you some lovely soup," his mum replied.

Harry crawled dramatically down the stairs to the kitchen table.

"**HMMPPHH**," he muttered.

He thought his mum was being mean.

"I'm just going to the toilet," his mum said after she put the soup on the table.

She quickly left the room.

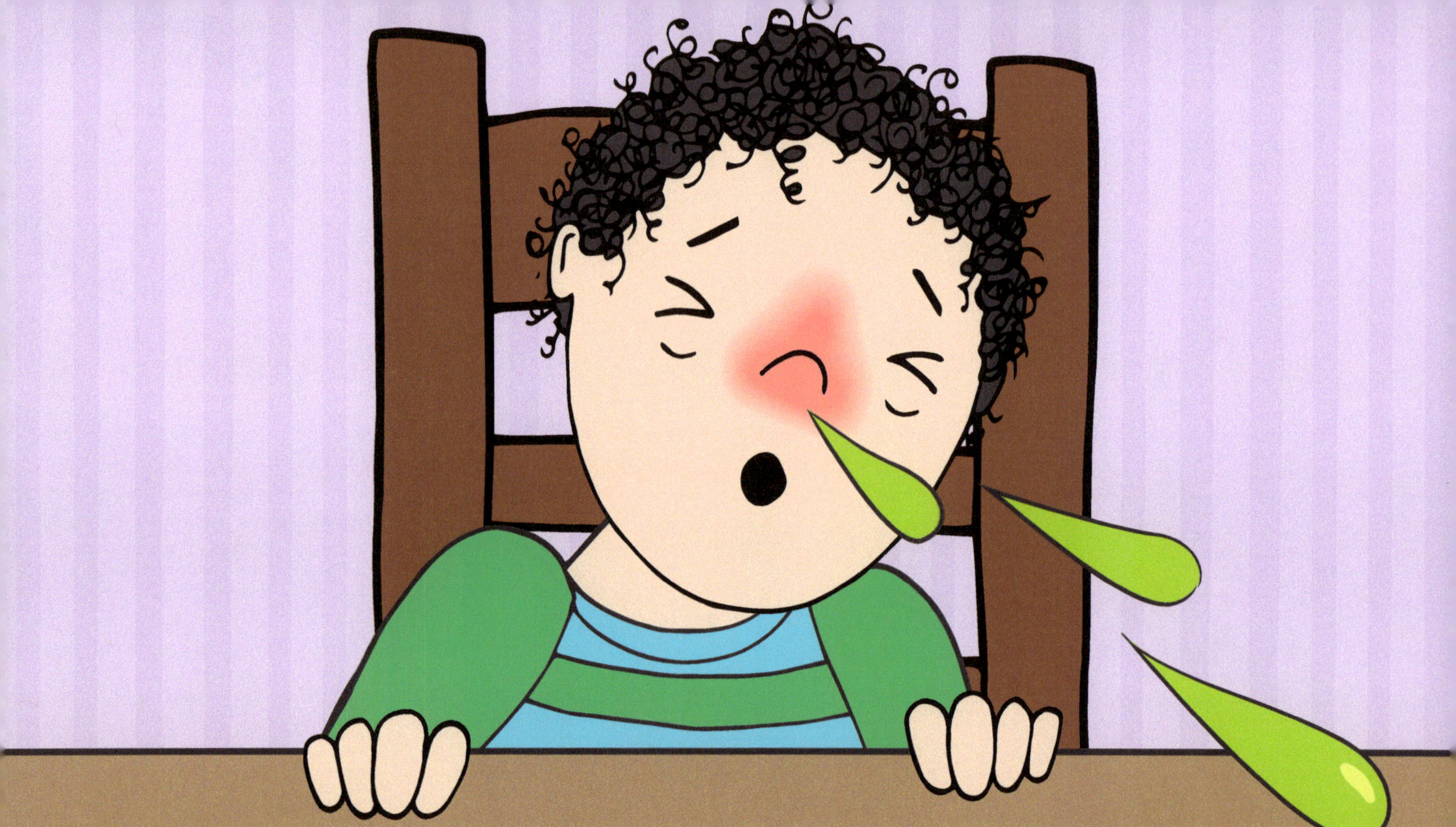

Harry could feel a really, really, REALLY big sneeze coming.

AAAHHH...

AAAAAAHHH...

AAAAAAAAHHH...

...CHOOOOOOOOOOOOOOOOOOOOOOOOOO!

Huge blobs of green snot flew out of his nose and landed **PLOP** straight into the soup!

Harry and Hotdog looked at each other with shock on their faces.

"This soup looks delicious,"
his mum said, as she stepped back into the kitchen.

As mum poured the soup she said.
"You'll feel a lot better once you have some of this soup in your tummy.
How odd, it looks thicker than usual. Not to worry..."

I bet it still tastes **AMAAAAAAAZING.**"

Harry and Hotdog looked like they were going to be sick as they watched the snot bobbing around.

He watched his mum put the spoon towards her mouth, thinking he should let her eat it because she was mean to him earlier.

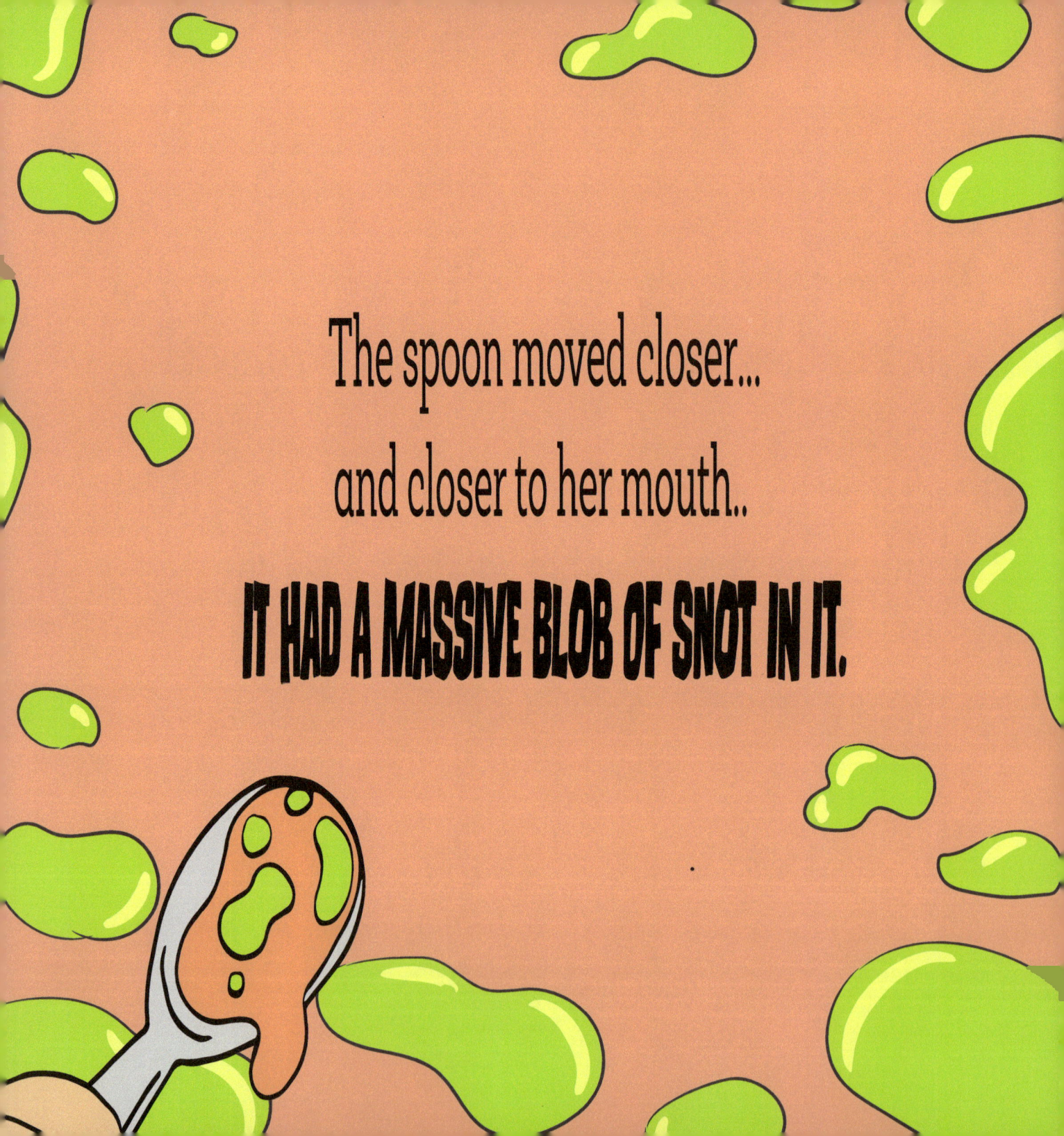

STOP!

He couldn't let his mum eat it. He loved his mum.

DON'T EAT THE SOUP!

"Why not?" asked his mum.

"I sneezed and my snot flew into it."

AAAAARRRRCCCHHHOOOOOO!

He sneezed again, straight into the soup.

"Put your hands over your mouth when you sneeze. Euurrgghhh, snotty soup!" she said, smiling at him. "I'm so glad you told me. Who wants to eat snotty soup, eh?."

STOP!

His mum stood up and poured the soup into an empty jar.

"I'll put it in the bin once it's not as hot."

His mum opened the window and placed it on the ledge to help it cool down.

"Come on, let's get snuggled on the settee and watch your favourite cartoon."

Not long after a naughty robber walked past their house. What's that delightful aroma? he thought.

He sneakily popped his head up to the window and did a massive sniff.

"Oooooh, I reckon that's pea soup," he whispered.

He watched the green blobs swirling around. He couldn't wait to eat it. His stomach growled. He looked around to check if anyone was watching. All was clear.

He reached up and quickly grabbed the jar.
Hotdog started barking.

"Go away, silly dog," he whispered angrily.
The robber tiptoed to the street and then ran as fast as he could all the way home.

He slammed the door behind him and put the jar on his table.

Today he had stolen a child's sandwich and a teenager's ice cream, but this soup just smelled and looked so delicious he was hungry all over again.

He gave the soup a stir with his spoon.

The green 'peas' bobbed around. He managed to get the biggest gloop and slowly put it into his mouth...

He did a big gulp as it all went down his throat.

"**YUMMY**" he shouted to himself and finished the rest of the soup off chasing all the 'peas' around the jar.

He ate so much that he quickly fell asleep on the settee.

ROBBER ROBBER, ALL MY SOUP HE GOT,

Harry and his mum finished watching their cartoon and went into the kitchen to make something to eat.

"Oh!" his mum suddenly said.

"Where has the soup gone?"

"I don't know mummy, maybe Hotdog ate it?" Harry replied.

They both looked at Hotdog and Hotdog looked at them. She put her paw to her mouth like she was going to be sick.

"No, Hotdog wouldn't eat my snot. She's not silly," Harry replied, giving her head a little pat.

"Oh dear, a robber must have stolen it!"

ROBBER ROBBER, EATEN ALL MY SNOT,

"Mummy, we can watch our house cameras back and see what happened."

They both watched the robber creep up the garden path and steal the soup.

"Robber robber, all my soup he got,
Robber robber, eaten all my snot,
He's a snot robberrrrrrrrrrrrr...
He's a snot robberrrrrrrrrrrrr..."

Harry sang, dancing around the room.

Meanwhile... the robber had woken up from his nap and his stomach hurt and he felt sick.

"**BLURRGGGHHH!**" he groaned.

He needed help. He ran outside his house and was sick all over the pavement, just as a policeman was walking past.

Meanwhile, Harry and his mum passed close by as they were walking to the shops, and spotted the robber on the path.

"Well, well, well," the policeman said.
"What do we have here then?"

The robber was rolling about on the floor. "I'm not very well!"

"Mum" Harry said.
"That must be the robber who stole our soup!"

The robber heard Harry.
"What was in the soup?" he moaned.

Harry and his mum looked at each other and smiled, then they laughed, and then laughed some more.

"Looks like I am going to arrest you for stealing," the policeman said to the robber.

"WHAT WAS IN THE SOUP?" the robber whimpered.

"**MY SNOT!**" Harry shouted and started laughing again. "I sneezed into the soup, twice. We were going to throw it away!"

Harry, his mum, and the policeman started laughing.

"Robber robber, all my soup he got,
Robber robber, eaten all my snot,
He's a snot robberrrrrrrrrrrrr,
He's a snot robberrrrrrrrrrrrr!"

Harry sang again.

"I think eating snot is punishment enough," the policeman said, in between laughing.

As the robbers face went even greener they all sang together:

SNOT ROBBBERRRRRRRRRRR!

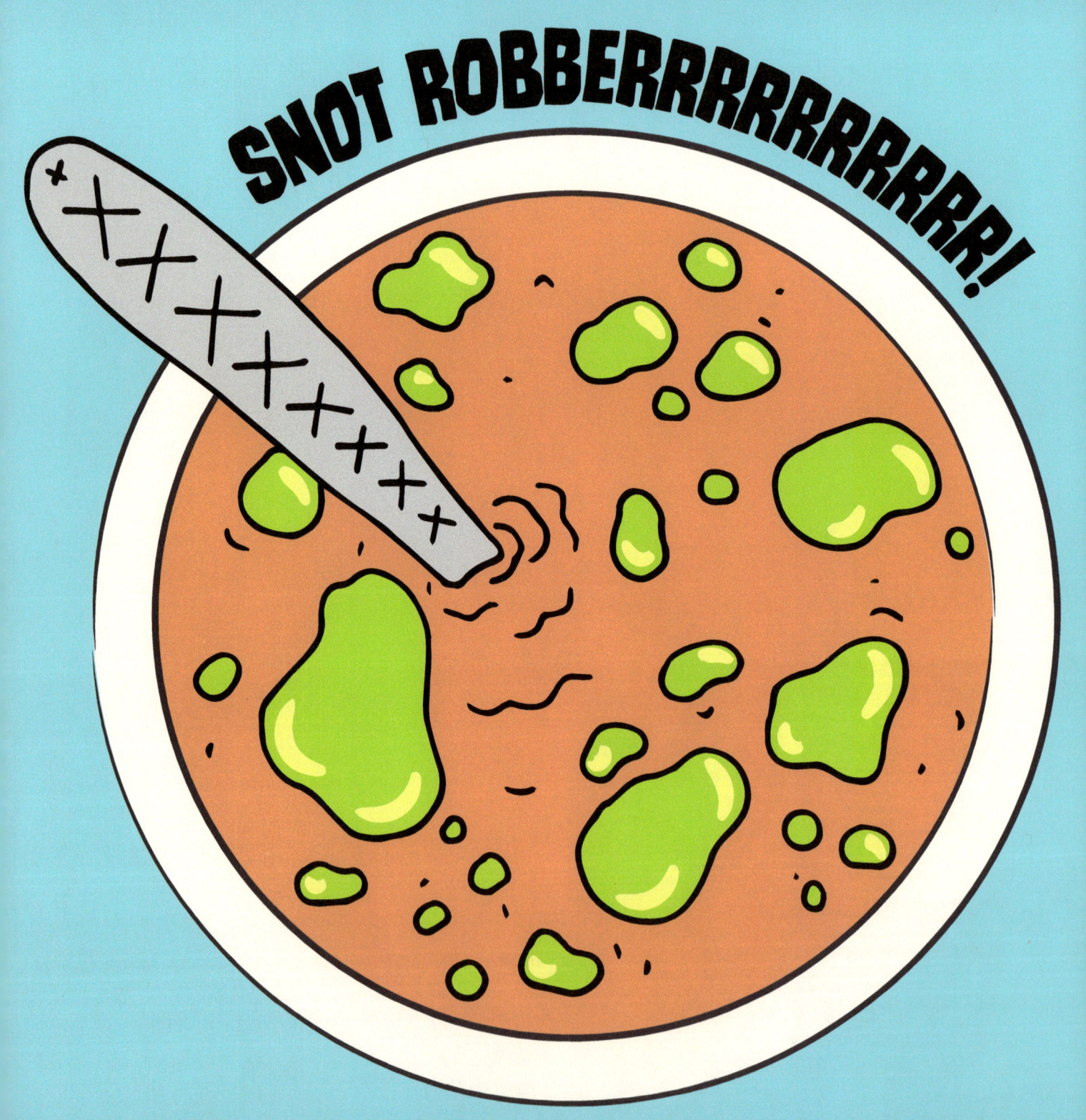

SNOTTY SOUP

♪ lynseycalvertauthor

f Lynsey Calvert Author

📷 lynseycalvertauthor

✉ lcalvert1977@gmail.com

www.ingramcontent.com/pod-product-compliance
Lightning Source LLC
Chambersburg PA
CBHW041122070526
44584CB00002B/243